Table of Contents

INTRODUCTION	2
CHAPTER 1: INTRODUCTION TO VIDEOGRAPHY	4
CHAPTER 2: EQUIPMENT ESSENTIALS	6
CHAPTER 3: UNDERSTANDING VIDEO SETTINGS	8
CHAPTER 4: COMPOSITION AND STORYTELLING	10
CHAPTER 5: AUDIO IN VIDEOGRAPHY	12
CHAPTER 6: SHOOTING TECHNIQUES	14
CHAPTER 7: EDITING AND POST-PRODUCTION	16
CHAPTER 8: DISTRIBUTION AND MARKETING	18
CHAPTER 9: PROFESSIONAL DEVELOPMENT	20
CHAPTER 10: FUTURE TRENDS IN VIDEOGRAPHY	22
CONCLUSION	24

Chapter 1: Introduction to Videography

1. What is videography?

Videography means capturing moving images with a camera. It's used for events like weddings, birthdays, or for making videos for businesses and art projects.

2. How is videography different from filmmaking?

Filmmaking is bigger, with stories, scripts, and larger teams. Videography is simpler and often records events or makes videos for specific needs without much planning.

3. Why is videography important today?

Video is a great way to share messages and grab attention online. Platforms like YouTube and TikTok make video a key tool for businesses, teachers, and creators.

4. What types of videography are there?

Different videography types include:

Event Videography: Recording weddings or parties.
Documentary Videography: Real-life stories.
Corporate Videography: Videos for businesses.
Commercial Videography: Ads for products.
Artistic Videography: Creative and experimental.
Educational Videography: Teaching and learning videos.

Chapter 2: Equipment Essentials

1. What do I need to start videography?

You need:

Camera: DSLR, mirrorless, or even a good smartphone.
Tripod: For stable and smooth shots.
Microphone: For clear audio.
Lighting: LED panels or softboxes for better visuals.
Editing Software: Tools like iMovie or Adobe Premiere Pro to edit videos.

2. How do I choose the right camera?

Think about:

Budget: Spend what you can afford.
Use: Choose based on what you'll film (e.g., action, events).
Portability: For travel, a smaller camera is better.
Lenses: Pick a camera with good lens options.

3. What lenses are good for videography?

Standard Zoom (24-70mm): For versatile shots.
Prime (50mm f/1.8): Great in low light and for blurry backgrounds.
Wide-Angle (16-35mm): Best for landscapes or tight spaces.
Telephoto (70-200mm): For faraway subjects.

4. Do I need accessories like tripods and stabilizers?

Videography Q&A

by

Pinnacle Press

Introduction

Welcome to **Videography Q&A**! This guide is designed to help anyone interested in making great videos, whether you are just starting out or already have experience. Videography is more than just filming. It combines technical skills, creativity, and storytelling.

The book is written in a question-and-answer format, making it easy to find useful tips. It covers the basics of videography, including equipment and simple shooting techniques. You will also learn about technical skills like settings, editing, and how to use sound effectively. The guide explains how to create interesting videos by combining visuals and sound to tell a strong story. There are also tips for sharing your work and building your brand. Additionally, it looks at new technology and career opportunities in the field.

Videography Q&A is for anyone who wants to improve their video skills. Every videographer has a unique story to share, and this guide will help you tell yours. Pick up your camera and start your journey into videography!

Yes, these accessories can help:

Tripod: Keeps shots steady.
Gimbal: Smooths out handheld shots.
External Monitor: Makes it easier to see and focus.
ND Filters: For shooting in bright light without overexposing.

5. How can I budget for videography equipment?

To budget for videography equipment:

Research: Compare prices and read reviews.
Prioritize: Buy the must-haves first.
Buy Used: Save money with second-hand gear in good condition.
Set Limits: Stick to your budget and plan ahead.

Chapter 3: Understanding Video Settings

1. What is frame rate, and why does it matter?

Frame rate is how many images (frames) are captured per second in a video:

24 fps: Film-like look, used in movies.
30 fps: Smoother, common for TV and online videos.
60 fps: Very smooth, good for sports and action.

Higher frame rates can also be slowed down for cool slow-motion effects.

2. How do I pick the right resolution for my videos?

Resolution decides how clear your video looks:

HD (720p): Great for simple online videos.
Full HD (1080p): Standard for high-quality video.
4K (2160p): Super detailed, best for professional work.

Keep in mind, higher resolutions need more storage and better editing tools.

3. What is bit rate, and why is compression important?

Bit rate: How much data your video uses per second. Higher bit rate = better quality but bigger files.
Compression: Shrinks file size by removing data but might lower quality.

Finding a balance gives you good quality without giant files.

3. How do I adjust exposure, aperture, and ISO for video?

Aperture (f-stop): Controls light. Lower f-stop (e.g., f/2.8) makes bright shots with blurry backgrounds. Higher f-stop (e.g., f/16) keeps everything in focus.

ISO: Sets how sensitive your camera is to light. Use low ISO (100) for bright places, high ISO (1600) for dark ones, but higher ISO can add grain.

Shutter Speed: Usually double your frame rate (e.g., 1/50 for 24 fps) for smooth motion.

Adjust these based on lighting to get the right look for your video.

Chapter 4: Composition and Storytelling

1. What is video composition, and what are its main principles?

Video composition is how elements are arranged in the frame. Key principles include:

Rule of Thirds: Divide the frame into a 3x3 grid. Place subjects on the lines or intersections.
Leading Lines: Use lines in the scene (roads, paths) to guide the viewer's eye.
Framing: Surround your subject with natural elements (like a window or tree) to focus attention.
Balance: Evenly spread visual weight in the shot.
Depth: Add layers with a foreground, middle ground, and background for a 3D feel.

2. How do I tell a good story with video?

Focus on these steps:

Clear Concept: Know your main idea or message.
Structure: Start with an intro, add development/conflict, and finish with a resolution.
Visual Metaphors: Use imagery to represent bigger ideas.
Emotions: Choose visuals, music, and pacing to match the mood you want.
Editing: Use cuts, transitions, and pacing to keep the story engaging.

3. Why is lighting important in videography?

Lighting sets the mood, tone, and clarity of your video:

Natural Light: Shoot during the golden hour (after sunrise or before sunset) for soft light.
Three-Point Lighting: Use a key light, fill light, and backlight for a balanced look.
Mood: Soft light feels warm, while harsh shadows add drama.
Color Temperature: Warm tones (low Kelvin) feel cozy; cool tones (high Kelvin) feel clinical or intense.

4. How do I frame shots for the best impact?

Use these tips:

Close-ups: Show details or emotions up close.
Wide Shots: Set the scene with a full view of the environment.
Over-the-Shoulder: Show a scene from behind a character for connection.
POV Shots: Let the viewer see what the character sees.
Dynamic Angles: Try high, low, or tilted angles for visual interest.

Chapter 5: Audio in Videography

1. Why is audio quality important in videos?

Good audio makes your video more engaging and professional:

Clear Dialogue: Helps viewers understand speech or interviews.
Emotional Impact: Sound effects and music add mood and feeling.
Professionalism: Crisp audio shows attention to detail and quality.

2. What microphones should I use for different situations?

Lavalier Mics: Clip-on, perfect for interviews or dialogue.
Shotgun Mics: Directional, great for isolating voices outdoors.
Handheld Mics: Good for live events or on-the-go interviews.
Condenser Mics: Best for studio work or voiceovers.
Field Recorders: Capture high-quality audio separately from the camera.

3. How can I reduce background noise while filming?

Pick Quiet Locations: Avoid noisy areas like streets or crowded places.
Use Directional Mics: Focus on the sound you want to capture.
Add Windshields: Reduce wind noise outdoors.
Monitor Audio: Use headphones to catch problems while filming.
Soundproofing: Use rugs, curtains, or panels to absorb unwanted noise.

4. What software can I use to edit audio?

Adobe Audition: For professional editing and noise reduction.
Audacity: Free and simple for basic audio fixes.
GarageBand: Easy for Mac users to mix music and sounds.
Final Cut Pro/Adobe Premiere Pro: Video editors with built-in audio tools.
Logic Pro: Advanced software for detailed soundtracks and editing.

Chapter 6: Shooting Techniques

1. What are some basic camera movements to learn?

Here are essential camera movements:

Panning: Moving the camera side to side for following action or revealing a scene.
Tilting: Moving the camera up or down to show tall subjects or add scale.
Dolly Shots: Physically moving closer or further from the subject for depth and focus.
Tracking Shots: Following a moving subject to keep the viewer engaged.
Crane Shots: Using a crane or jib to get dramatic, high-angle views.
Handheld Shots: Adds raw, intimate energy but needs steady control.

2. How do I plan a successful shoot?

Follow these steps:

Shot List: Write down every shot you need to capture.
Storyboard: Sketch or describe key scenes to plan visuals.
Scout Locations: Visit locations to check lighting and sound.
Rehearse: Practice with your subjects to ease nerves and improve performance.
Prepare Gear: Charge batteries, clear memory cards, and bring extras.

3. Why are shot lists and storyboards important?

Shot lists and storyboards help by:

Organizing Your Vision: Keep track of your creative ideas.
Improving Communication: Make sure your team knows the plan.
Saving Time: Work faster and avoid missing important shots.
Boosting Creativity: Plan different angles and compositions.

4. How can I direct subjects effectively on camera?

Use these tips:

Build Trust: Help your subjects feel relaxed and confident.
Be Clear: Use simple, specific instructions.
Encourage Naturalness: Let them act naturally or improvise when possible.
Give Feedback: Offer helpful and kind suggestions to improve performance.
Be Patient: Stay calm and supportive to reduce stress.

Chapter 7: Editing and Post-Production

1. What is the best video editing software?

The best video editing software depends on your needs and experience:

Adobe Premiere Pro: Professional and feature-packed, works for all levels.
Final Cut Pro: Powerful and user-friendly for Mac users.
DaVinci Resolve: Great for color grading, with a free version available.
iMovie: Easy and free for Mac users, ideal for beginners.
HitFilm Express: Free, with editing and visual effects for experimenting.

2. How do I organize footage for editing?

To organize footage for editing:

Make a Project Folder: Include subfolders for video, audio, graphics, and project files.
Label Clips: Use clear names like "Scene1_Take2_Date."
Add Metadata: Keywords and descriptions help sort clips in your software.
Create Bins: Organize clips into folders by scene, type, or location.
Backup Files: Save copies on an external drive or cloud storage.

3. What are key editing techniques to learn?

Key editing techniques to learn include:

Cutting and Trimming: Keep pacing smooth and remove unnecessary footage.
Color Correction and Grading: Adjust colors for consistency and mood.
Titles and Graphics: Add clear and stylish text for context.
Transitions: Use fades or cuts sparingly to maintain flow.
Sound Editing: Balance audio, remove noise, and add music or effects.

4. How do I improve my video with color grading and effects?

Here are ways to improve your video with color grading and effects:

Color Grading: Adjust color, contrast, and saturation for a polished look.
Use LUTs: Apply pre-set color profiles for consistent and professional results.
Add Effects Sparingly: Enhance the story without overwhelming it.
Layer Creatively: Blend footage, effects, and graphics for depth.
Get Feedback: Share your work for fresh opinions and ideas.

Chapter 8: Distribution and Marketing

1. What platforms are best for sharing videos?

YouTube: Best for reaching a large audience, monetization, and long-form content.
Social Media: Use platforms like Instagram, TikTok, Facebook, or LinkedIn for short, engaging content.
Your Website: Showcase your videos with full control over branding and style.
Streaming Services: Submit longer, scripted content to platforms like Amazon Prime Video.

2. How do I optimize my videos for SEO on YouTube?

This is how to optimize your videos for SEO on YouTube:

Keywords: Use tools to find relevant keywords and include them in your title, description, and tags.
Titles: Make them catchy and clear with important keywords.
Descriptions: Write 200+ word summaries with keywords and links to related content.
Custom Thumbnails: Use eye-catching images that match your video.
Engage Viewers: Ask for likes, comments, and subscriptions to boost rankings.

3. What are good marketing strategies for videographers?

Here are good marketing strategies for videographers:

Social Media: Share highlights, teasers, and interact with your audience.
Networking: Meet industry professionals through events and forums.
Collaborations: Work with creators or businesses to reach new audiences.
Email Lists: Send newsletters about projects and offers.
Portfolio Website: Display your best work professionally and make it easy for clients to contact you.

4. How do I build a portfolio to attract clients?

To build a portfolio to attract clients:

Show Your Best Work: Focus on quality, not quantity.
Diverse Projects: Include different styles and genres to show versatility.
Case Studies: Explain your process and outcomes for select projects.
Professional Layout: Use clean designs with high-quality visuals.
Keep It Updated: Add recent work and remove outdated pieces regularly.

Chapter 9: Professional Development

1. How can I improve my videography skills?

To improve your videography skills:

Take Online Courses: Learn from platforms like Skillshare, Udemy, or YouTube.
Practice Often: Experiment with different projects and techniques.
Get Feedback: Share your work with peers or mentors for constructive criticism.
Attend Workshops: Join workshops or seminars for hands-on learning.
Stay Current: Follow blogs, podcasts, and industry news to learn about trends and tools.

2. What resources can help me learn videography?

Books: "The Filmmaker's Handbook" or "Cinematography: Theory and Practice."
Courses: Try Coursera, MasterClass, or CreativeLive for expert lessons.
YouTube: Watch channels like Film Riot, Peter McKinnon, or DSLR Video Shooter.
Communities: Join Reddit's r/videography or Facebook filmmaking groups.
Networking Events: Look for local meetups, film festivals, or online groups.

3. How do I network with other videographers?

Attend Events: Go to film festivals, trade shows, or conferences.
Join Groups: Become part of professional organizations or local filmmaker groups.
Social Media: Connect on LinkedIn, Instagram, or Twitter by sharing and engaging.
Collaborate: Work with others on joint projects to build skills and connections.
Follow Up: Stay in touch after meeting someone to maintain the relationship.

4. What are the career paths in videography?

Career paths in videography include:

Freelance Videographer: Take on various projects like weddings and corporate videos.
Corporate Videographer: Create branding and marketing videos for a company.
Documentary Filmmaker: Focus on real-life stories and impactful topics.
Commercial Videographer: Produce advertisements and promotional materials.
Cinematographer: Work in film or TV to create the project's visual style.
Video Editor: Edit and assemble footage into the final product.
Content Creator: Build your own brand on YouTube or social media.

Chapter 10: Future Trends in Videography

1. What emerging technologies are shaping videography?

4K and Higher Resolutions: 4K is standard, and 8K is emerging, offering more detail and editing flexibility.
360-Degree Video and VR: Immersive storytelling and training applications are gaining popularity.
Drones: Affordable drones make aerial videography accessible and creative.
AI in Editing: Automates tasks like color correction and sound mixing, improving efficiency.
Live Streaming: Growing demand for high-quality real-time content on platforms like YouTube Live and Twitch.

2. How is VR changing videography?

Here are ways VR is changing videography:

New Storytelling: Allows viewers to study environments and interact with stories.
Rising Demand: More industries (gaming, education, tourism) need VR content.
Skill Development: Videographers must learn 3D modeling and spatial audio.
Stronger Engagement: Offers a personal, immersive way to connect with viewers.

3. How does social media influence videography?

Social media can influence videography in the following ways:

Short-Form Content: TikTok and Instagram Reels demand quick, attention-grabbing videos.
Audience Interaction: Engage directly through comments, shares, and live sessions.
Real-Time Feedback: Understand viewer preferences and refine your craft.
Viral Opportunities: Unique content can reach large audiences quickly.

4. How can videographers adapt to industry changes?

Videographers can adapt to industry changes by:

Staying Updated: Following trends and learning about new technologies.
Lifelong Learning: Taking courses and attending workshops to enhance skills.
Experimenting: Trying new formats like live streaming and interactive videos.
Networking: Collaborating with professionals working on cutting-edge projects.
Being Flexible: Welcoming changes and adapting to new standards and tools.

Conclusion

As we finish this journey into videography, it's important to reflect on what we've learned. Videography is more than capturing video; it's a mix of technical skills, creativity, and storytelling. Whether you're starting your first project or refining your expertise, the ideas and techniques in this book can help you improve your work.

Key lessons include the importance of ongoing learning. Videography constantly changes, so staying curious and learning new skills through courses, workshops, or practice is essential. Technical skills, like understanding your equipment and mastering video settings and editing, are key to creating high-quality content. Storytelling is at the core of videography. Through visuals, lighting, and audio, you can connect with your audience and share meaningful stories.

Building connections with other videographers can inspire you and open new opportunities. Joining communities, both online and offline, allows you to share knowledge and grow together. Flexibility is also crucial, as trends and tools in the industry keep changing. Trying new styles and platforms will help you connect with your audience in fresh ways.

Every project is a chance to learn and create something meaningful. Stay true to your vision and don't hesitate to try new ideas. This book aims to give you the tools and inspiration to take your videography to the next level, whether you want to create stunning videos, promote a brand, or capture life's special moments.

Thank you for being part of this journey. We can't wait to see the amazing videos you will create!

www.ingramcontent.com/pod-product-compliance
Lightning Source LLC
Chambersburg PA
CBHW070946220526
45469CB00007B/2534